THE SPACE EXPLORER'S GUIDE TO

Mars

...in 3-D!

BY
BILL DOYLE

WITH
MARIANNE DYSON
TECHNICAL CONSULTANT

RYAN WYATT
VISUAL ADVISOR

AND
JIM SWEITZER, PH.D.
NASA SCIENCE CENTER, DePAUL UNIVERSITY

Use your 3-D glasses
to view this image.

SCHOLASTIC INC.

NEW YORK   TORONTO   LONDON   AUCKLAND   SYDNEY
MEXICO CITY   NEW DELHI   HONG KONG   BUENOS AIRES

Bill Doyle
Writer

Bill is a writer who lives in New York City. He has written for Sesame Workshop, TIME for Kids, the Discovery Channel, Leapfrog, and the American Museum of Natural History.

Marianne Dyson
Consultant

Marianne is a former NASA mission controller and award-winning nonfiction author who dreams of touring the galaxy.

Ryan Wyatt
Visual Advisor

Ryan designs scientific visuals for the American Museum of Natural History's Rose Center for Earth and Space.

Jim Sweitzer
Advisor

Jim is an astrophysicist and the director of the NASA Space Science Center at DePaul University in Chicago.

With special thanks to:

Dr. Geoff Landis, Dr. Chris McKay, Dr. Heather Sloan, Donna Shirley, and Jim Sharp

ISBN: 0-439-55748-8

Copyright © 2004 by Scholastic Inc.

Editor: Andrea Menotti
Assistant Editor: Megan Gendell
Designers: Peggy Gardner, Lee Kaplan, Tricia Kleinot, Robert Rath
Illustrators: Yancey C. Labat, Ed Shems

Photos:
Front cover: Mars as seen from the *Mars Global Surveyor* (NASA/JPL/MSSS)
Back cover: The *Mars Global Surveyor* orbiting Mars (NASA/JPL)
Title page: One of the MER rovers that landed on Mars in 2004

Title page image and MER images on pages 21, 27 to 31, and 36 (unless otherwise noted) are from an animation by Dan Maas, Maas Digital LLC, © 2002 Cornell University. All rights reserved. This work was performed for the Jet Propulsion Laboratory, California Institute of Technology, sponsored by the United States Government under Prime Contract # NAS7-1407 between the California Institute of Technology and NASA. Copyright and other rights in the design drawings of the Mars Exploration Rover are held by the California Institute of Technology (Caltech)/ Jet Propulsion Laboratory (JPL). Use of the MER design has been provided to Cornell courtesy of NASA, JPL, and Caltech.

All other images are NASA/JPL unless otherwise noted.

Pages 4 and 5: (Mars landscape) NASA/JPL/Cornell. Page 5: (volcano) John Mead/Photo Researchers; (Death Valley and Mono Lake) Simon Fraser/Photo Researchers; (Arctic) NASA Haughton-Mars Project/SpaceRef.com. Page 10: (crater) NASA/JPL/Cornell. Pages 10 and 11: (global Mars) NASA/JPL/MSSS; (Earth) NASA. Pages 12, 17, and 21: (global Mars) NASA/USGS. Page 12: (Phobos) NASA/JPL/MSSS. Page 13: NASA/Calvin J. Hamilton. Page 16: NASA/Photo Researchers. Page 17: (Valles Marineris close-ups) NASA/USGS. Page 18: (ice caps) NASA and The Hubble Heritage Team (STScI/AURA); (Happy Face, sand dunes, and gully) NASA/JPL/MSSS; (craters) NASA/JPL/Arizona State University. Page 19: (bottom) NASA/JPL/MSSS. Page 20: (*Mars 1*) Sovfoto/Eastfoto; (*Mariner 9* and *Viking*) NASA; (*Mars 2*) Courtesy of the Planetary Society. Page 21: (*Mars Global Surveyor*) NASA/JPL/MSSS; (*Mars Express*) ESA. Page 24: (rover) NASA/JPL/Caltech; (Sojourner Truth) Library of Congress, Prints & Photographs Division. Page 26: Courtesy of Donna Shirley. Page 28: (packing rover) NASA/JPL/KSC; (*Delta II*) NASA. Page 29: (empty lander) NASA/JPL/Cornell. Page 30: (*Sojourner*) Daniel Maas/Maas Digital LLC, Cornell, NASA/JPL. Pages 32 and 33 (Earth rocks) The Atlas and Glossary of Primary Sedimentary Structures, by Francis John Pettijohn and Paul Edwin Potter, plates 20B, 29B, and 32A, 1964, Springer-Verlag. Pages 33 and 34: (Mars rocks) NASA/JPL/Cornell/USGS. Page 34: (photo 1) Sinclair Stammers/Photo Researchers; (photos 2 and 3) Heather Sloan. Page 40: (Dr. Landis) Barbara Sprungman; (*Sojourner*) NASA/JPL. Page 41: (Lowell and map) Photo Researchers; (*Viking*) NASA. Page 42: (meteorite close-up) NASA/ARC. Page 43: Library of Congress, Prints & Photographs Division, Carl Von Vechton collection. Page 45: Pat Rawlings. Pages 46 and 47: (terraformed Mars) Paul Bourke, Centre for Astrophysics and Supercomputing, Swinburne University. Page 47: (Dr. McKay) Courtesy of Dr. McKay.

3-D conversions by Jim Sharp (Pinsharp 3-D Graphics)

12 11 10 9 8 7 6 5 4 3 2 1

4 5 6 7 8 9/0

Printed in the U.S.A.

First Scholastic printing, August 2004

The publisher has made every effort to ensure that the activities in this book are safe when done as instructed. Adults should provide guidance and supervision whenever the activity requires.

Table of Contents **Contents**

Welcome

You might find Mars a little chilly on the surface, cadet—but you're [in for] a warm Red Planet welcome from the entire Martian population...

In this new phase of your Space University training, you'll take a c[lose] tour of our closest neighbor—a planet that's been fascinating Earthli[ngs for] centuries. You'll explore questions like:

- How does Mars stack up against Earth? Which planet is bigger? Warmer? Wetter? *Rustier?*

- What's the weather like on the Red Planet[?]

- How do we know that Mars used to have sea[s?]

- Is there life or evidence of life on Mars?

- Why do we keep sending so many probes to check out the Red Planet, and how many have actually made it there?

- When will humans be able to travel to Mar[s?]

- How long would it take to get to Mars?

- What would it be like to *live* on Mars?

The Martian sky is pinkish-orange during the midday because of dust particles in the atmosphere.

MARS!

So, what's in store for your Red Planet tour? You might be surprised to find that there are some spots on Mars that could remind you of home!

MARS ON EARTH!

Here are just a few Mars-like spots on Earth. Scientists actually visit and study places like these to prepare for Mars missions!

Aloha, cadet! The Hawaiian islands have lots of extinct volcanoes like the kind you'll find on Mars. Burst to page 13 for more on Red Planet top-blowers!

In California's Death Valley, the desert environment has geological features like the craters and hills on the Red Planet. For more on Martian surface features, check out pages 17–19!

Dig below the surface of chilly spots up in the Arctic, and you'll find frozen water that's a bit like the ice found in Mars's polar ice caps. To get cracking on more icy facts, slide over to page 18!

A 700,000-year-old lake in California called Mono Lake fills a basin that's similar to Mars's Gusev Crater. Did *Gusev* once hold water? Try the mission on page 32 to find out!

SEE THE SIGHTS...IN 3-D!

Your Red Planet tour will be *anything* but flat and boring, cadet—you'll see Mars in three amazing dimensions, like you're really there!

So, are you ready for a real eye-popping tour? Then turn the page to get started!

A view of the Martian surface as seen by the rover *Opportunity*. See page 27 for more on this rover and its twin, *Spirit*!

WHAT'S IN THIS MONTH'S SPACE CASE?

Your Mars adventure would not be complete without a brand new Space Case! Here's what you'll find inside:

■ **A build-your-own rover kit.**
Construct your own rover, power it up, and test it out on Mars-like terrain! Rove on over to page 37 to start the wheels turning!

■ **3-D glasses.** You'll need these eye-enhancers to check out the cool 3-D images throughout this book. To find out how your glasses work their magic, head over to page 7 (right next door)!

3-D Alert!

Look for this symbol throughout the book. Whenever you spot it, pop on your new glasses to experience Mars in 3-D!

THE SPACE UNIVERSITY WEB SITE

Cadet, you have been granted clearance to Space U's official Mars web site! You can guide a rover around Martian terrain, find out how to run *your* new rover with solar power, and more! Just be sure to bring this month's password when you rocket off to www.scholastic.com/space!

Complete all the games and challenges on the Space U web site to earn this month's mission patch. Show it off by pasting it right here!

PLANET PASSWORD
This month's web site password is:
REDPLANET

3-D THRILLS

What makes flat images appear to pop out from the page when you pop on your 3-D glasses? Read on to find out!

SEEING DOUBLE

Take a look at the pictures below. They may look the same at first glance—but if you look carefully, you'll notice slight differences in the positions of objects (the rover's antenna looks closer to the rock beside it in the right image, for example). That's because these two images show the scene from slightly different viewpoints—one for each of your eyes!

Human eyes are about $2\frac{1}{2}$ inches (6 cm) apart (on average), so they take in different views. When your brain puts the two views together, the differences between them help it determine information like distance and shape. That's how we see the world in 3-D!

QuickBlast

3-D Eye Test

Want proof that your eyes see different views? Try this:

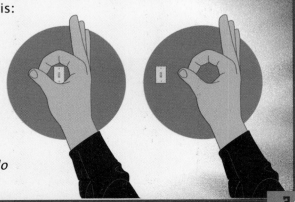

1 With your left eye closed, make an O with your thumb and forefinger and hold it up so that something across the room is inside that O, like a light switch on the opposite wall.

2 Without moving your hand, open your left eye and close your *right* eye. The object should no longer be inside the O!

Your eyes don't seem very far apart, but they really *do* see different views of the world!

To get a better *eye*-dea of how we see in 3-D, get two toilet paper tubes or roll up two pieces of paper to create two tubes. Hold a tube in front of each eye and look at the images of the rovers on the previous page. Your left eye should see only the *left* image through its tube, and your right eye should see only the *right* image through its tube. Make sure the image is centered inside each tube.

Now, relax your eyes and let the two images merge. When they do, you'll see one image, in 3-D! The rover should pop out in front, and the rocks should look like they're off in the distance. That's because your brain is combining the images it gets from each eye to create one 3-D image! If you can't see the image in 3-D, try moving farther away. Keep trying and be patient! And if you really *can't* see the 3-D, just move on (this technique doesn't work for everyone).

EYE-POPPING IMAGES

To create 3-D images on paper, each of your eyes has to see a slightly different picture, just like they do when you're looking at a three-dimensional scene in real life. One way to show each eye a different picture involves overlapping red and blue images, which can be looked at through special red-and-blue 3-D glasses (grab *your* pair from your Space Case now!).

Take a look at the images below. They're the same two images you saw on the previous page, but this time one is all blue and the other is all red.

Wearing your 3-D glasses, cover your right eye. You should be able to see this image clearly. Now, cover your left eye and look at the image with just your right eye. The image will fade away! That's because when you look at the color blue through the blue filter over your right eye, the color essentially disappears!

While wearing your 3-D glasses, you should see this image clearly with your right eye, but it will seem to vanish when you look at it with just your left eye.

So how can these images give you a 3-D view? When they're printed right on top of each other, both of your eyes can look at the same place at the same time (so no need to use tubes like you had to before!). But, thanks to your glasses, your right eye will see only the red image, and your left eye will see only the blue image. You brain combines the slightly different images received by each eye to create one 3-D image—just like in real life!

 Once the images are completely overlapped, they pop into 3-D when you look through your glasses!

QuickBlast

Your Words in 3-D

For more fun with 3-D, write a message on top of the image below. Now put on your 3-D glasses and see what happens to your words! On this month's Space U web site (www.scholastic.com/space), you'll find some great 3-D stationery just like this. Print it out and use it to write letters to your friends!

Part 1: Gusty, Dusty, and Just Plain Rusty

Mars is all about extremes! Everything about it is either too cold, too dry, or too windy. From the second you step off your spacecraft onto the Martian surface, you'll know you're in a very hostile (and deadly!) environment. To make your stay more pleasant, Space U's Department of Red Planet Tourism presents...

THE TOP **5** TRAVEL TIPS FOR VISITING MARS!

TIP #1: JUMP FOR JOY!

Even if you're tired after the seven-month trip from Earth, you'll still feel light on your feet! That's because Martian gravity is about a third of Earth's—so on Mars you'll weigh about a third of your current weight!

TIP #2: GET GASSY!

Thanks to Mars's low gravity, the air on Mars is very thin (lower gravity means the Red Planet can't hang on to gases as well as Earth can).

Unlike Earth's air, which contains enough oxygen for humans to breathe, Mars's air is made of about 95 percent carbon dioxide. So, make sure you've got gas when you get to Mars—the right *kind* of gas, that is!

 Why is the Martian surface reddish, cadet? One word: RUST! Iron in Mars's soil has rusted, giving the whole place a reddish look.

TIP #3: BRING WARM CLOTHES!

If you hate hot weather, cadet, then you won't have *anything* to complain about on Mars! At its warmest, Mars can reach 63 degrees F (17 degrees C), which is about the same as a brisk fall day on Earth. But the *average* temperature on Mars is more like –81 degrees F (–63 degrees C), and temps can plunge to –184 degrees F (–120 degrees C)!

To roam around the Martian surface, you'll need to wear a nice, insulated suit with breathing equipment (see Tip #2) and sturdy boots to tackle the rocky terrain!

TIP #4: BE SURE TO GO WITH H₂O!

Don't forget to pack some water for your trip to the Red Planet! Mars doesn't have oceans, rivers, or lakes (at least *nowadays* it doesn't). Most of the water on Mars freezes around the poles of the planet and forms the polar ice caps. Some ice is also locked in the Martian soil, and there's a tiny bit of water vapor in the air.

TIP #5: WATCH OUT FOR DUST STORMS!

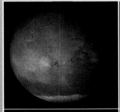 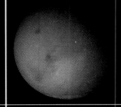

Before Dust Storm | During Dust Storm

Martian winds can crank up to 186 miles per hour (300 km/h). Sounds pretty blustery, doesn't it, cadet? But don't worry—*you* won't get blown over because the air on Mars is really thin (so the wind will feel like a breeze). Dust, on the other hand, will get blown everywhere!

When the winds *really* get whirling, Mars can have full-fledged dust storms that last for months! These storms turn the sky pink as dust swirls in the air.

Mars vs. Earth

How does the Red Planet stack up against Earth? Check out this chart to find out!

	Mars	Earth
Distance from Sun	142 million miles (228 million km)	93 million miles (150 million km)
Diameter	4,220 miles (6,791 km)	7,926 miles (12,756 km)
Length of Year	687 Earth days	365.25 days
Length of Day	24 hours 39 minutes	24 hours
Gravity	.38 that of Earth	2.7 times that of Mars
Average Temperature	–81 degrees F (–63 degrees C)	57 degrees F (14 degrees C)
Number of Moons	2	1
Atmosphere	95% Carbon dioxide 2.7% Nitrogen 1.6% Argon Tiny amounts of oxygen and other gases	78% Nitrogen 21% Oxygen 1% Water vapor, carbon dioxide, and other gases

Who's Hanging Out Around MARS?

Mars has two tiny moons with scary names: Phobos (Greek for "fear") and Deimos ("terror" or "panic").

Not to fear, this dynamic duo is dinky! Phobos is about 14 miles (23 km) wide, and Deimos is only about 7.5 miles (12 km) wide. That's pretty tiny compared to Earth's Moon, which has a diameter of 2,159 miles (3,475 km).

Scientists think these mini-moons, which were discovered in 1877, are actually asteroids that were captured by Mars's gravity.

Mars and its moon Phobos

Cadet Travel Tip

If you make it to Deimos, be sure to bring your bike. There's so little gravity on Deimos that riding a bike up a ramp is enough to send you free-floating in space!

KING of the MOUNTAINS

A trip to Mars wouldn't be complete without a peek at Olympus Mons, the largest known volcano in the solar system. This mammoth mountain is 17 miles (27 km) high—around three times the height of Mt. Everest—and 374 miles (624 km) across, covering about the same area as the state of Arizona!

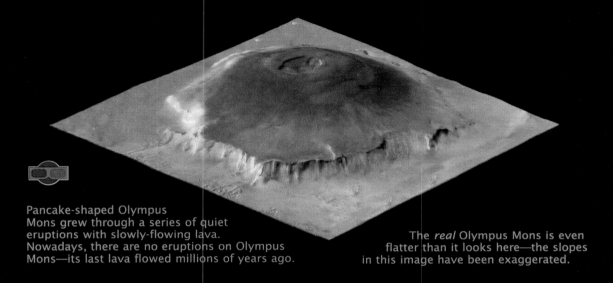

Pancake-shaped Olympus Mons grew through a series of quiet eruptions with slowly-flowing lava. Nowadays, there are no eruptions on Olympus Mons—its last lava flowed millions of years ago.

The *real* Olympus Mons is even flatter than it looks here—the slopes in this image have been exaggerated.

WHO CAN GROW THE BIGGER VOLCANO?

Why can't Earth cut it in a volcano-growing competition with Mars? It's all about the crust. Earth's crust is broken into pieces or "tectonic plates" that float on the hot, liquid rock underneath.

A volcano forms when pressure builds up deep below the surface, pushing the liquid rock up through the crust. As the melted rock (or *lava*) continues to flow and harden, the volcano grows bigger. But then, on Earth, the plates move and carry away the volcano before it can grow to Olympus Mons proportions. The crust on Mars doesn't move very much—meaning layer after layer of lava can build up until the volcano is a solar system giant. To see how this works, try the next mission!

Earth's crust is made of plates that slowly drift on top of the melted rock underneath. Volcanoes form where the plates meet.

MARS

It's been millions of years since Mars's Olympus Mons last blew its top. (See page 13 for more on this mega-mountain!) Got a love for lava and don't feel like waiting to see if the "Mons" will ever erupt again? Then construct your own colossal 'cano!

Launch Objective

▷ **Build a working volcano!**

Your equipment

▶ **Paper towels**
▶ **Four handfuls of play dough, clay, or your own volcano dough (see Part 1)**
▶ **Scissors**
▶ **Small paper cup**
▶ **Large piece of stiff cardboard**
▶ **Tape**
▶ **1 cup (240 ml) baking soda**
▶ **Measuring cup**
▶ **1 cup vinegar**
▶ **Red food coloring**
▶ **Pencil**
▶ **Spoon**

Personnel

▶ **An Intergalactic Adult (IGA)**

Mission Procedure

To begin, find yourself a good workspace and cover any stainable surfaces with paper towels (because you'll be working with food coloring). Make sure to get 'cano construction clearance from an IGA!

Part 1: Ready, Set...Dough!

If you already have play dough, skip ahead to Part 2. If not, follow these instructions to make your own volcano dough!

> **You'll Need:**
> - $\frac{2}{3}$ cup (160 ml) water
> - Red and green food coloring
> - Large mixing bowl
> - $1\frac{1}{2}$ cups (360 ml) flour
> - 1 cup salt
> - Spoon

1 Add equal amounts of red and green food coloring to the water until it turns brown. Be careful not to drip food coloring on your hands or clothes—it'll stain! (But once the coloring is mixed into the dough, you don't have to worry.)

2 Mix the flour and salt together in a large bowl.

3 Stir in the water a little at a time until the dough is just the right consistency for kneading and modeling. Test the dough by grabbing a handful and trying to form a shape with it. If the dough is too dry and lumpy, add more water. If it's too wet and sticky, add more flour.

Part 2: Create Your 'Cano

1 Divide your dough (or clay) into four equal portions. Each portion should be about the size of a lemon.

2 Cut the cup so it's only 1 inch (2.5 cm) tall and tape it to the center of the cardboard.

3 Roll one portion of the dough into a "snake" and wrap it around the cup. Press the dough

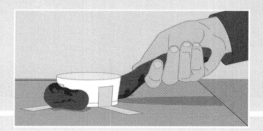

with your thumbs to make a lumpy hill around the cup. Make sure there's no gap between the rim of the cup and the dough.

4 Fill the volcano's cup two-thirds full of baking soda.

5 Now make some red lava for your 'cano! Pour the vinegar into a measuring cup and add one or two drops of red food coloring.

6 Ready for an eruption? Then shout, "Mars she blows!" and slowly pour the red vinegar into the baking soda. Stop pouring as soon as the cup starts to overflow!

7 Once the eruption is over, mark the edges of the lava flow by poking small holes with a pencil in the volcano dough, leaving a dotted line. In places where the lava flowed onto

the cardboard, just draw a pencil line to mark the eruption area.

8 Blot the lava with a paper towel and use a spoon to scoop out the remaining baking soda and vinegar from the cup.

9 Using another portion of your volcano dough, cover the eruption area. Sculpt the layer of dough so it matches your outlined area exactly. If you have any extra

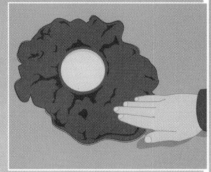

dough when you're done, add it to one of your remaining portions.

10 Repeat steps 6–9 twice. When you're done, spoon out the remaining baking soda and vinegar and wipe the cup clean with a paper towel. If you'd like to keep your Olympus Mons, let it dry for at least two days (until it hardens).

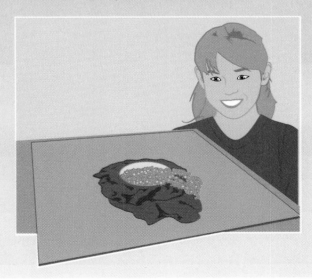

Deep below the surface of a soon-to-blow volcano, an underground chamber of melted rock and hot gases is bubbling away. Finally, the pressure from the gases forces the molten rock up to the surface, where the lava erupts!

The same kind of thing happens inside *your* volcano. When you add the red vinegar to the baking soda in your cup or "underground chamber," the chemical reaction creates bubbles of carbon dioxide. These bubbles push the "lava" up and out of the cup in a "volcanic eruption"!

As you learned on page 13, each time a volcano erupts, the lava cools and hardens, adding to the size of the volcano. You built your 'cano the same way—adding layers of dough to represent hardened lava.

There are different kinds of volcanoes—some with thick, rocky lava, and others with thin, fluid lava. The second kind are called "shield volcanoes," and Olympus Mons is one of these. Remember its pancake shape? That's because it formed from flow after flow of lava drying in thin sheets on its surface. Volcanoes that look like cones are formed from explosive eruptions of thicker lava.

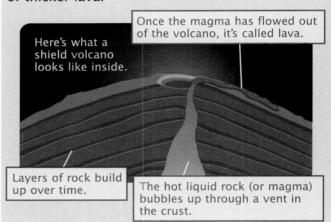

Here's what a shield volcano looks like inside.

Once the magma has flowed out of the volcano, it's called lava.

Layers of rock build up over time.

The hot liquid rock (or magma) bubbles up through a vent in the crust.

Mauna Loa is a shield volcano on one of the Hawaiian islands. Notice how its shape is similar to Olympus Mons!

GRANDEST CANYON

S o, cadet, now that you've explored Mars's highest mountain, it's time to get
the *lowdown* on another Red Planet sensation: Valles Marineris!

HOW LOW CAN YOU GO?

Valles Marineris is a set of canyons that makes the Earth's Grand
Canyon look like a minor scratch. It's more than 4 miles
(7 km) deep in places (that's deep enough to swallow up
the entire Alps mountain range), and about 2,500
miles (4,000 km) long (it would stretch all the way
across the United States)!

Valles Marineris ———

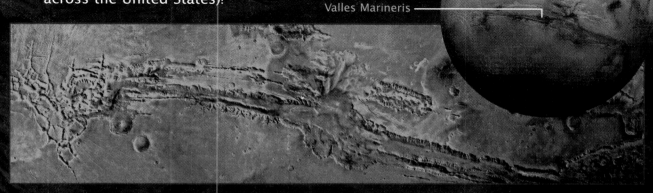

 Valles Marineris began as a series of big cracks in Mars's crust that gradually grew wider.
The canyon was also shaped by wind and water erosion, as well as by landslides.
The slopes shown in the image below look steeper than they are in real life.

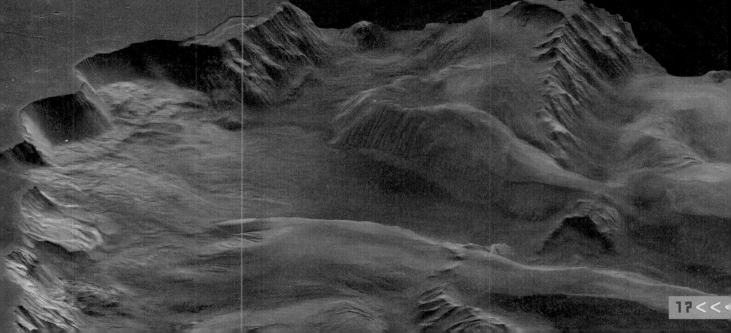

You Look MARS-ELOUS!

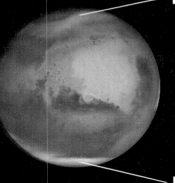

Ice cap

Ice cap

W hat other cool features does the Red Planet have to offer?

▶ **Polar ice caps:** Carbon dioxide ice, dust, and water ice form ice caps on both Mars's north and south poles. The ice caps shrink in the summer when the carbon dioxide ice evaporates.

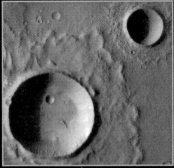

This crater is known as the Happy Face Crater—can you see why?

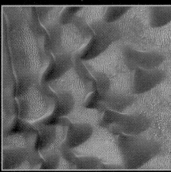

◀ **Impact craters:** These are left behind when meteorites (huge rocks) from space smash into the Martian surface. Most of Mars's craters were formed 3.8 billion years ago when Mars was bombarded with lots and lots of meteorites.

◀ **Sand dunes:** Wind helps shape sand dunes like these in the dusty Martian surface.

▶ **Channels and gullies:** Mars has lots of channels and gullies that look like they were formed by flowing water!

FACE the TRUTH

 ure, you can see FACE in the word SURFACE...but can you see a face on the surface of Mars?

On July 25, 1976, NASA's *Viking 1* orbiter was looking for a great spot for a spacecraft to land when it snapped the shot you see below.

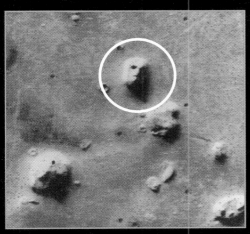

What does the circled part look like to you, cadet? A face, right? Well, you're not alone. Many people back on Earth thought this mile-long raised area was actually a sculpture of a face constructed by aliens who wanted to send us a message. These people referred to it as the Face (with a capital F!).

But NASA experts were Skeptical (with a capital S). They explained that the Face was probably just a trick of light and shadows on a rippled hill.

 It wasn't until 1998 when the *Mars Global Surveyor* sent back the image below that the truth was known for certain.

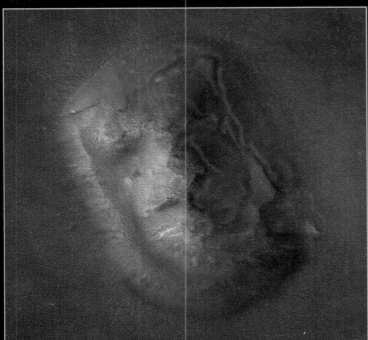

Unfortunately for those who wanted to prove the existence of aliens, NASA was right all along. The Face was just a mesa—a flat-topped hill with steep sides. Light, ripples, and dust had created the illusion of the Face!

Part 2:
Probe the Red Planet

Earthlings have sent lots of orbiters, landers, and rovers to check out the Red Planet over the years. The timeline below shows you only the missions that made it past Earth's orbit—many more didn't make it that far!

Mars 1

[Th]e Soviet [sp]acecraft *Mars 1* was [su]pposed to fly by [M]ars, but partway there [th]e spacecraft stopped [co]mmunicating with [Ear]th.

Mariner 9

Mariner 9 orbited Mars and returned thousands of photos, revealing gigantic volcanoes, the Martian moons Phobos and Deimos, Mars's huge Valles Marineris canyon (which was named after *Mariner*), and much more!

Viking 1 and Viking 2

Viking 1 and *Viking 2* were orbiters with landers, which performed the first experiments on Mars's surface. Altogethe[r] the *Viking* orbiters and landers returned much information all previous Ameri[can] missions to Mars combined—more than 50,000 phot[os]

1962   **1964**   **1965**   **1969**   **1971**   **1973**   **1975**

[Z]ond 2

[Zo]nd 2 flew [by] Mars, but [co]mmunications [fai]led along the way, [ju]st as they had with [Ma]rs 1. This caused [Am]erican engineers [to] joke that there [wa]s a "great galactic [gh]oul" that ate up [sp]acecraft!

Zond 3

Zond 3 flew past our Moon to take pictures before flying by Mars. It was the first Soviet spacecraft to make it past Mars without getting lost!

Mars 2 and Mars 3

These two spacecraft were equipped to orbit Mars and send down landers with rovers. *Mars 2* sent the first lander down to Mars, but it crashed. The *Mars 3* lander made it down safely, but it went silent after twenty seconds—it may have been blown over by winds from huge dust storms at the time.

Mars 2's rover

Mars 4, 5, 6, and 7

Mars 4, 5, 6, and *7* were not very successf[ul] missions. *Mars 4,* an orbiter with a faulty computer chip, couldn'[t] slow down to orbit Mar[s,] so it flew right past (b[ut] fortunately it sent hom[e] some pictures!). *Mars 5* managed to orbit Mars and send back some information and picture[s,] but it went silent after nine days. *Mars 6* and *Mars 7* both carried lande[rs,] but neither lander made [it] to the surface successful[ly.]

[M]ariner 4

[M]ariner 4 was the first [sp]acecraft to successfully fly [pa]st Mars. It sent back our very [fir]st views of the surface of the Red Planet!

One of the twenty-two images *Mariner 4* sent back to Earth

Mariner 6 and Mariner 7

These two spacecraft flew by Mars and studied its surface and atmosphere. They passed over the equator and the poles, transmitting 201 photos of Mars to Earth.

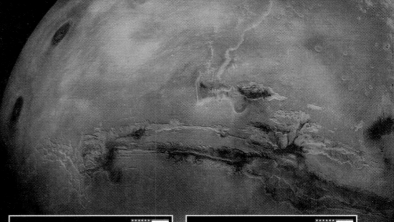

Mars Global Surveyor

The *Mars Global Surveyor* orbiter arrived at Mars in 1997 to map the surface, study the composition of rocks, monitor Martian weather, and examine the planet's magnetic field.

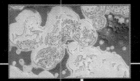

Mars Climate Orbiter

Mars Climate Orbiter tried to orbit Mars—but instead crashed into the Red Planet because of a mix-up with measurements! The people making the orbiter for NASA had used *English* units of measure (like inches), while NASA had used *metric* units (like meters) to program the orbiter!

Mars Odyssey

Mars Odyssey arrived at Mars in 2001 to map the planet's surface and to study the radiation on Mars, which will help scientists understand how to make a trip to Mars safe for humans in the future!

Mars Observer

Mars Observer, an orbiter, was sent to study the surface and atmosphere of Mars. It suddenly lost contact with Earth just before it tried to begin its orbit.

1988   **1992**   **1996**   **1998**   **1999**   **2001**   **2003**

Phobos 1 and Phobos 2

Phobos 1 and *Phobos 2* were orbiters that carried landers meant to touch down on Mars's moon Phobos. *Phobos 1* got lost on the way to Mars because a scientist transmitted a message missing one character, causing the spacecraft to point its solar arrays the wrong way and lose power. *Phobos 2* was lost near Phobos before it could release its two landers.

Mars Pathfinder

The *Mars Pathfinder* lander and its rover, *Sojourner*, arrived on Mars in 1997 and returned much more information and images than expected—more than 16,000 images from the lander and 550 images from the rover!

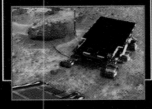

Nozomi

Nozomi, a Mars orbiter sent by Japan, flew past Mars and went into orbit around the Sun!

Mars Express

The *Mars Express* orbiter and lander (*Beagle 2*), sent by the European Union, made it to Mars, but the lander was lost as it descended through the Martian atmosphere.

Mars Polar Lander

The *Mars Polar Lander* contained probes to drill for water in the Martian south pole, but unfortunately, the lander crashed upon arrival.

Mars Exploration Rover (MER)

The twin MER rovers, *Spirit* and *Opportunity*, arrived on Mars in January 2004 to analyze rocks and soil. Rove over to page 27 to find out more about their discoveries!

This timeline shows the year each mission was launched.

This Finder's a Keeper!

The *Sojourner* rover on Mars

On July 4, 1997, NASA's *Mars Pathfinder* became the first spacecraft to land successfully on the Red Planet in more than twenty years. (*Viking 1* and *Viking 2* had made the last landings way back in 1976.)

The *Pathfinder* lander deployed the rover *Sojourner*, and for almost three months, this little rover collected data on rocks, soil, and Martian weather. *Sojourner* also performed experiments to help future lander/rover combos make the most of their time on the Red Planet.

ABOVE AND BEYOND!

Originally, the purpose of *Pathfinder* was just to see if a lander and rover could be sent to Mars successfully. But *Pathfinder* wowed the world beyond anyone's expectations, sending back tons of data and lasting much longer than planned. (Instead of one month, the mission lasted almost *three* months, ending when the lander's battery could no longer recharge itself.)

What did we learn from *Pathfinder*? Instruments on both the lander and the rover picked up evidence that Mars was once a warmer place, where water existed in a liquid state!

Pathfinder was a stellar success, but the mission wasn't smooth sailing from the beginning. Read on to find out about some obstacles it had to overcome before it made it to Mars!

In this patch for the *Pathfinder* mission, you can see what the rover and lander might have looked like on Mars.

MARS
PATHFINDER

NASA · JPL

How to Clear Obstacles in Your **Pathfinder**

Pathfinder scientists had to think fast when problems came up during the spacecraft's seven-month trip to Mars. Here are two big ones that could have ruined the whole mission!

1 The *Pathfinder* spacecraft had a sunlight sensor that helped it position itself in relation to the Sun—but shortly after launch, NASA engineers realized that *Pathfinder* was ignoring readings from the sensor. They soon figured out that soot from the launch must have been blocking some of the sunlight. Without these sunlight readings, *Pathfinder* could go off course.

THINK FAST: What would you do, cadet?

Here's what NASA did: Scientists realized that *some* sunlight was still getting through. So NASA just told *Pathfinder* to accept lower levels of light to determine the position of the Sun. But when they tried to send these commands to the spacecraft, a new problem cropped up....

Pathfinder arrives at Mars after its seven-month trip.

2 *Pathfinder* wouldn't accept NASA's commands! Scientists also noticed a mysterious dip in the signal from *Pathfinder* every five minutes. They finally figured out that the signal dip happened when the spinning spacecraft turned its antenna away from Earth, which broke contact with Mission Control. The break in contact meant that *Pathfinder* couldn't receive commands properly!

THINK FAST: What would you do, cadet?

Here's what NASA did: Scientists decided to send signals at a much slower rate, so that when the antenna was turned away from Earth, it would miss only a little information instead of a whole lot. Then, *Pathfinder* could use its error-correction software to fill in the information it missed. And sure enough—*Pathfinder* accepted commands, and the problem was solved!

When *Pathfinder* landed safely on Mars, the rover *Sojourner* came rolling out, ready for its Martian debut! Here's a breakdown of its features.

Antenna: This was the rover's means of communication with the lander.

Material Adherence Experiment: This sensor helped scientists learn about the dust on Mars.

Solar Panel: This provided the rover with energy.

Alpha Proton X-Ray Spectrometer: Using this instrument, the rover could analyze the elements in Martian rocks.

Cameras: These allowed the rover to see where it was going and to send photos back to Earth.

Rocker-Bogie Mobility System: The wheels were attached to this rocking frame to allow the rover to scramble over rocks.

Warm Electronics Box: The rover's electronics were kept insulated inside this box so they wouldn't freeze in the cold Martian weather.

Before the launch of the *Pathfinder* mission, NASA held a worldwide contest asking kids to name the robotic rover. Valerie Ambroise, a twelve-year-old student from Connecticut, thought of the winning name: *Sojourner Truth*. In the 19th century, Sojourner Truth was a former slave who spoke out against slavery and in support of women's rights.

e That Rock

you believe there's a Martian named Yogi? A Martian *rock*, that is!
*nde*r scientists gave names to many of the rocks found in images
to Earth by the lander. You can see some of them in the photo below.

Turtle

Platypus

Yogi

Pop Tart

Dice

SA scientists named these rocks by writing their suggestions on sticky notes
placing them on a giant picture of the landing site. Then, every few days,
neone went through all the ideas and decided which of the names were keepers!

nes probably aren't as serious as you might have expected. While
uge planetary features like canyons and giant craters is taken very
scientists had a lot more fun naming these small rocks. They used
cartoon characters—like Yogi, Scooby Doo, and Stimpy—or gave the
nes that described their shapes—like Flat Top, Wedge, and Couch.

ready to be a rock star? We've left blanks for the names of some of the
s in the image below. Here's your chance to name them! When you're
n to page 48 to see the names the *Pathfinder* scientists gave them!

Donna Shirley
AEROSPACE ENGINEER

Donna Shirley stands in front of a model of the *Sojourner* rover.

Cadet, say hello to Donna Shirley! While working at NASA's Jet Propulsion Laboratory in Pasadena, California, Ms. Shirley led teams that designed missions to Mercury, Venus, Jupiter, Saturn, Uranus, Neptune—and, of course, Mars! She was in charge of the teams that built the *Sojourner* rover, and she managed the Mars Exploration Program, which included *Pathfinder*, the 1998 *Mars Global Surveyor*, and the 2001 *Mars Odyssey* orbiter.

Nowadays, Ms. Shirley is the director of the Science Fiction Museum and Hall of Fame in Seattle, Washington!

Question: How old were you when you first knew what you wanted to do?

Answer: I always wanted to be a pilot. When I was ten, I decided to be an aeronautical engineer and build airplanes. Later, when space travel started, I focused on that (from 1959 on).

Q: Why were you interested in space travel?

A: I was always fascinated with flying and read a lot of science fiction about exploring other planets when I was a teenager.

Q: What was the most exciting aspect of working on the *Pathfinder* mission?

A: Doing something that had never been done before—landing on Mars for a tenth of the cost of *Viking* and sending the first rover to explore another planet.

Q: What was the most challenging aspect?

A: Staying within budget!

Q: What did you contribute to *Sojourner*'s design?

A: I was the team leader from 1992 to 1994. I recruited the staff, led the planning and design activities (that doesn't mean I *did* the design—it's a team effort), negotiated and protected the budget, and "sold" the rover to the public and to NASA.

Q: What were some of the big technical hurdles you had to overcome?

A: Probably the biggest technical hurdle was weight—keeping everything on the rover and lander light enough to be launched on a low-cost launch vehicle.

Q: How did you feel as you waited to find out if *Pathfinder* would land safely and send back a signal?

A: I was very, very nervous. The night before the landing, I didn't sleep well. I had a dream in which I saw the *Pathfinder* team standing around in a field when suddenly our spacecraft fell from the sky before us. It had landed on Earth!

Q: What would you have done if *Pathfinder* hadn't landed safely on Mars?

A: Cried a lot and focused on the next mission!

Q: What do you think future Mars rovers should be able to do?

A: Go farther, carry more instruments, go to more challenging places, and drill into the surface to try to detect water!

The SPIRIT and the OPPORTUNITY to EXPLORE MARS!

In January 2004, six and a half years after *Sojourner* first set wheels on the Martian surface, the *next* Mars rover landed on the Red Planet—not once, but *twice*! Cadet, meet the twin *Mars Exploration Rovers*, *Spirit* and *Opportunity*!

Fully loaded with high-tech instruments, these two golf-cart-sized rovers (*Sojourner* was the size of a microwave oven!) were launched separately and sent to different locations. Each location was carefully selected by scientists who thought the two sites would be great places to hunt for evidence of Mars's long-gone liquid water. Check out the next few pages to get the scoop on this mission—and to examine the clues the rovers sent home!

This image was created for an animated video showing what the *Spirit* and *Opportunity* rovers might look like on Mars. To see the complete video of the rovers in action, check out the Space U web site!

The JOURNEY Begins...

A fter many years of design, construction, and testing, *Spirit* and *Opportunity* were ready for launch in the summer of 2003.

The NASA technicians you see here are covered in protective suits so they won't contaminate the rover with Earthling bacteria. If the rover brought bacteria from Earth, it could multiply on Mars and hurt our chances of figuring out if Martian life ever existed on its own.

PACK FOR THE TRIP

First, each rover needed to be carefully packed inside its spacecraft. The rover folded up to fit inside the lander, and then the lander's "petals" closed around it.

3...2...1...MARS!

Each rover was launched on top of a *Delta II* rocket, and then, after seven-month journeys, *Spirit* and *Opportunity* arrived at Mars!

Spirit and *Opportunity* were protected by heat shields as they fell down through the Martian atmosphere. Then, like *Pathfinder*, they used rocket engines and parachutes to slow their fall and bounced to a safe landing surrounded by lots of airbags. Check out page 36 for more on this!

Ready to ROVE!

After the lander stopped bouncing and rolling and its airbags deflated, the petals of the lander opened, revealing the folded-up rover inside. Time to rock the Red Planet!

The rover's solar panels opened and the antenna popped up...

...and then the wheels folded out.

The images above were part of the rover video mentioned on page 27. Below, you can see an actual photo of the lander taken by the *Spirit* rover on Mars!

The rover's empty nest!

SUPER ROVERS!

What special features make *Spirit* and *Opportunity* such rockin' rovers? Check 'em out!

Cameras for navigation and for taking wide panoramic photos of Mars

Low-gain antenna as a backup if the high-gain antenna can't communicate

Solar arrays

Microscopic imager to study rocks up close

High-gain antenna to communicate with Earth

Alpha-particle X-ray spectrometer to learn about the composition of rocks

Rock-abrasion tool to chip away at the surface of a rock so the rover can study what's below

Leaving Others in the Martian Dust

Sojourner

Here's how *Spirit* and *Opportunity* compare to *Sojourner* from *Pathfinder*:

	SOJOURNER	SPIRIT and OPPORTUNITY
Mission Purpose:	To hunt for signs of life and test out a rover on the Martian surface	To search for signs of water and life
Launched:	December 4, 1996	*Spirit* launched on June 10, 2003; *Opportunity* on July 7, 2003
Landed:	July 4, 1997	*Spirit*: January 4, 2004; *Opportunity*: January 25, 2004
Communication:	Communication equipment was on the lander, so the rover could never get farther than 39 feet (12 m) from the lander—or it would risk losing communication.	Communication equipment was built onto the rover, enabling the rover to travel far from the lander!
Speed:	.025 miles per hour (.04 km/h)	.1 miles per hour (.16 km/h)
Instruments:	Three cameras and one robotic arm to test rocks and soil	Nine cameras and four different instruments to study rocks and soil

ROCK AROUND THE CLOCK

Spirit and *Opportunity* were designed to be real hard-core rock researchers, with scraping tools, drills, and analysis equipment!

 The rock-abrasion tool, or "RAT," was designed to dig into rocks to get samples from inside.

 The rover examines a rock with its rock-abrasion tool.

QuickBlast

Something "Bunny" Is Going On!

The two rovers returned all sorts of great images to Earth. Some contained exciting clues to the puzzle of Mars's past (as you'll see in the next mission)—and *other* photos turned out to be pretty puzzling themselves! Check out this Martian image of "bunny ears" photographed by *Opportunity*. Can you guess what this object actually is?

A) A sign that rabbits live on Mars

B) A piece of *Opportunity*'s airbag material

C) A strangely-shaped rock

D) A leaf from a Martian plant

Hop on over to page 48 for the answer!

MARS ROCKS!

Mission Procedure

Part 1: The Story Behind the Stone

Each photo below shows a section of a rock from Earth. Notice all the lines in each rock? Those are clues to how the rock formed. Geologists trace over these lines with darker marks to help them see major patterns.

Take a look at the lines a geologist drew to "interpret" or analyze the rocks below. Then, grab a colored pencil and interpret a rock from Mars!

This rock was formed by wind.

Notice how the lines in the rock go in all different directions? This tells us that the rock was created by wind, which can often change direction. You can see that the lines form very steep angles, too—this is another sign of a wind-formed rock.

This rock was formed by fast-flowing water.

Notice how there are two layers of rock here, each with many downward-sloping parallel lines? Those sloping lines tell geologists that the rock was formed by water flowing rapidly from left to right. As the water flowed quickly along, its currents rolled against the bottom of the stream, leaving behind sediment (grains of rock) in slanting layers like you see here.

This rock was formed by water that flowed slowly.

The lines in the rock here are mostly flat and parallel to the rock's layers. That's because they're the result of shallow, slowly-flowing water. As the water flowed gently along, it dropped sediment in an even layer along the bottom of the stream.

Part 2: Interpreting Mars

1 inch (2.5 cm)

Now that you know what you can learn from interpreting rocks, test your skills on a *Martian* rock! Take a look at the above photo, taken by the *Opportunity* rover in Gusev Crater.

1 Interpret this rock like the examples in Part 1, tracing over the lines you see with a colored pencil.

2 Look at the lines you just drew and compare them to the lines in the Earth photos in Part 1. Which rock formation do they look the most like? Based on your comparison, can you figure out how this Martian rock was formed? Turn the page to find out!

Here you can see how geologists interpreted the Mars rock. Do the lines they drew look like yours?

Notice how the lines are mostly parallel within the layers? Just like in the third image from Part 1, this means the rock must have been formed by shallow, slowly-flowing water!

If flowing water formed this rock, then Gusev Crater must have once held water! This was a really exciting find for scientists on the MER mission—it was front-page news in March 2004!

Why so much excitement over Mars's watery past? Because—where there's liquid water, life can exist! So, *Opportunity*'s big discovery was encouraging news for anyone hoping to someday find evidence of life on Mars!

More from Mission Control

Did you notice the round shapes in the image above? Here's a closer view:

1 inch (2.5 cm)

Some call these round shapes "blueberries," but they're not blue, and they're definitely not berries! What are they? See if you can find out by comparing them to images from Earth again (on the right).

Based on your analysis, do you think the blueberries are *more* evidence that there was once water on Mars? *Rock* on over to page 48 for the answer!

1 These pebbles and rocks came from a dry desert, where they were worn away by wind.

2 These pebbles were formed at the bottom of a stream, shaped by rushing water.

3 These little balls, called "concretions," were formed by water seeping through sand in the Sahara Desert. They grew slowly, as the water evaporated and crystals formed around small stones or grains of sand.

EGG-CELLENT LANDING!

Getting your rover to Mars is only half the problem—now you have to land it safely on the surface! Try this mission to see how tricky that can be!

Launch Objective

Construct a system to carry an egg safely to the ground—without getting it **scrambled**!

Your equipment

▶ **Paper towels or newspaper**
▶ **Raw egg(s)**
▶ **Plastic bag**
▶ **Cushioning material (like cotton balls, packing peanuts, or bubble wrap)**
▶ **Tape**
▶ **Large sheet of tissue paper or plastic grocery bag**
▶ **Chair**

Personnel

▶ **An Intergalactic Adult (IGA)**

Mission Procedure

1 Not only is it an *egg-ceptional* idea to involve an IGA from the very beginning of this mission, it's a direct command from Space U Mission Control. Things might get messy! And that's no *yolk*!

2 With your IGA, find the right spot to perform this experiment. Pick an outside spot that's easy to clean up, or be sure to spread paper towels or newspaper in a wide area in the "landing zone."

3 If you don't want to worry about cleaning up the mess of a broken egg, you can place your egg inside a plastic bag and tie it shut. This will keep your rough landings from getting too messy, although your bag might leak if the egg breaks.

4 Now it's time to prepare your egg for landing! One way to help your egg reach the ground safely is to protect it with cushioning. Try taping some cushioning material to your egg, like cotton balls, packing peanuts, or bubble wrap. You can also make your own cushioning—what about small blown-up balloons or plastic bags filled with air?

5 Another great way to keep your egg in one piece is to slow down its fall with a parachute. Find some lightweight parachute material, like a big piece of tissue paper. Lay it flat on the ground and tape each of the four corners of your parachute to the egg. Or, attach the handles of a plastic grocery bag to your egg so the bag forms a parachute. Experiment with the materials you have around to see what works best.

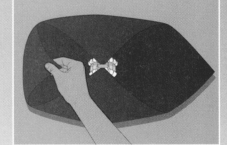

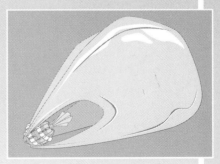

6 Now select a drop height. Start low and work your way up—for the first drop, stand on top of a chair.

7 Aim for the landing zone and release your rover!

8 Once your rover has landed, remove all the cushioning and check it out. How does it look?

A) "My rover made the drop with no cracks!"

Terrific! Now try dropping from a slightly higher spot, with help from an IGA. See how high you can get before your egg shows cracks or goes SPLAT!

B) SPLAT! "My rover is all over!"

Terrific! You're discovering how tricky it is to bring a rover in for a soft landing. Check out the questions below to see if the answers help keep your rover in one piece:

■ Did you drop the rover from too great of a height?

■ Can you surround the egg with a different kind of cushioning material? Or do you just need *more* cushioning?

■ Have you tried different kinds of parachute material? What if you make the parachute a different shape or create a bigger one? Would *two* parachutes help?

■ Was your parachute or cushioning material too heavy? The more weight your egg carries, the more force it will hit the ground with—so use the lightest materials you can find!

Science, Please!

By placing cushioning material around your egg and using a parachute to slow down its fall, your egg had a lot in common with the *Spirit* and *Opportunity* rovers sent to Mars!

Here's the story of *Spirit's* big drop:

After a seven-month trip from Earth, the *Spirit* rover, packed inside a lander for protection, was dropped off above Mars going about 12,000 miles per hour (19,000 km/h). *Spirit* plummeted to the surface for about four minutes, and then—when *Spirit* was about 6 miles (10 km) above the ground—a giant parachute opened up to slow down its fall.

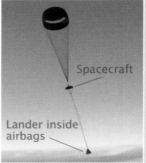

Spacecraft

Lander inside airbags

As the lander got closer to the ground, huge air bags inflated all around it. Then—and this is the coolest part—rockets fired to bring the lander to a dead stop about 40 feet (12 meters) above the ground.

Finally, the parachute was released and the lander dropped the rest of the way to the surface, where it bounced as high as four or five stories and rolled for several minutes before coming to a rest!

Then the airbags deflated and the lander opened up like the petals of a flower. Out rolled the *Spirit* rover, ready to begin its exploration of Mars!

Red Rover, Red Rover!

Now that you've learned all about roving on the Red Planet, grab the build-your-own rover kit from your Space Case and get ready to do some roving of your own!

Launch Objective

> **Build and test your rover!**

Your equipment

- **Build-your-own rover kit** Space Case
- **Screwdriver**
- **One AAA battery**
- **Measuring tape or ruler**
- **Masking tape**
- **Stopwatch or a watch with a second hand**
- **Hardcover book**
- **Small objects, like rocks, pencils, and erasers**
- **Heavy object, like a rock or soft-drink can**

Mission Procedure

Part 1: Putting It All Together

The first thing every space explorer has to do before using a rover is put it together! Just follow these steps:

1 Turn the rover upside down and press the rear wheels into place.

2 Loop the rubber band around the front wheel and press the wheel into place at the front of the rover.

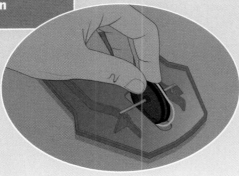

3 Flip the rover right side up. Align the motor with the slots on the rover and snap it into place.

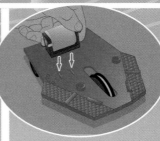

4 Connect the rubber band to the rod on the motor.

5 Open the battery compartment by pressing a screwdriver into the slot on one end.

6 Attach the battery plate to the top of the rover, making sure that the two (+) signs match up on one side and the (−) signs match up on the other side.

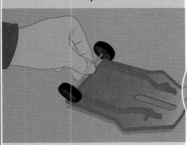

7 Secure the battery plate by dropping in screws from the top.

8 Holding the screws in place, flip over the rover.

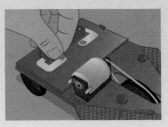

9 Place the loop at the end of the red wire over the screw marked with the (+), then twist a nut onto the screw to hold everything in place. Place the loop on the black wire over the (−) screw, and twist another nut onto that.

10 Insert an AAA battery, matching the (+) end (the end with a bump) with the (+) on the rover. Then place the lid on top of the battery plate and snap it in place.

11 Attach the antenna and camera to the top of the rover, and add your Space U sticker!

12 Now you're all set to power your rover! Just attach the free ends of the wires to the motor to turn on your rover. Make sure the red wire connects to the (+) side and the black wire connects to the (–) side. Or, connect the wires the opposite way and make your rover go backward! To turn off your rover, just remove one of the wires from the motor.

Part 2: Test Drive

Now that your rover is up and running, take it out for a test drive and clock its speed!

1 Find a flat surface—like a smooth floor or sidewalk. Mark a starting point with a piece of masking tape. Now measure 6 feet (2 m) and put down another piece of tape to mark the finish line. Way to go, cadet: You've just created a test track!

2 Attach the wires to the motor and hold your rover in front of the starting line. Release the rover and start the stopwatch at the same time.

3 Time how long it takes the front of the rover to cross over the finish line.

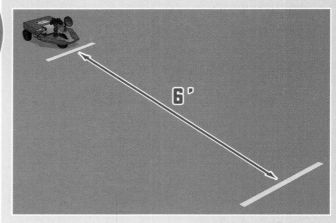

6'

4 To find your rover's speed, divide the distance by the time.

DISTANCE (FEET OR METERS)	÷	TIME (SECONDS)	=	SPEED (FEET OR METERS PER SECOND)

So, if your rover traveled 6 feet in 3 seconds, then its speed is 2 feet per second. What speed did *you* clock?

Part 3: Real Rover Challenges

How do you think your rover would do on Mars? Try these challenges to get an idea.

1 Try your rover out on hills. Find a big hardcover book and open its front cover. Start your rover a short distance away from the book and see if it can climb up the slope created by the open cover. Can your rover climb this tiny hill? If so, try lifting your book higher and

higher. How high can you lift the book before your rover can't make it up the hill? What changes would you make to your rover to help it manage steeper slopes?

2 Test your rover on an obstacle course.

Tape down small objects like rocks, pencils, and erasers to simulate the rocky terrain on Mars. Now release your rover and watch it try to tackle the terrain. Can it move over (or around) obstacles? Does it get stuck? Think about what changes you would make to your rover to help it deal with tough terrain!

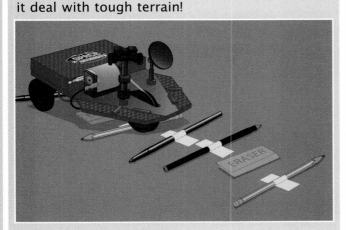

3 See if your rover can carry loads. Tape

something heavy on top of the rover, like a rock or a soft-drink can, then time the rover on its test track (from Part 2). How much did the extra weight slow your rover down? Try adding more and more weight and watch what happens!

Science, Please!

So, how does your rover compare to the real ones that rove around Mars?

You should have found that your rover took only about 2 seconds to complete its 6-foot course. The Mars rovers *Spirit* and *Opportunity*, on the other hand, would take about 40 seconds to get from one tape mark to the other! That's right—they're a lot slower, but keep in mind that each rover weighs 400 pounds (180 kg) and is about the size of a golf cart. You should have noticed that your rover couldn't go as fast once you added weight to it.

Did you also notice that if you lifted your book too high, your rover couldn't make it up the slope? Or did you find that your rover got blocked by rocks in its path? That's why the *Spirit* and *Opportunity* rovers are designed with cleats on their wheels to help them scramble up hills or over rocks and dusty surfaces. Their wheels can move up and down to help keep the rover balanced as it travels over rocks. And the wheels are all powered by separate motors so that if one gets stuck, the rest can keep moving and push the rover onward.

There's one other thing to consider about your rover, cadet: What will happen when its battery runs out? You can change the battery here on Earth, but if you sent that rover to Mars, you'd be out of luck! That's why the Mars rovers are powered by solar panels, which keep their batteries charged and allow the rover to run day or night! See the box below to find out how you can make *your* rover Sun-powered!

Sun-sational!

Want to power your rover with sunlight? Then rove over to this month's Space U web site at www.scholastic.com/space and print out the log pages. They'll tell you how to purchase and install a solar panel that will make your rover run on sunshine—no batteries required!

Solar panel

Dr. Geoff Landis

MARS ROVER SCIENTIST

Dr. Landis poses with a model of one of the *Mars Exploration Rovers.*

Cadet, meet rover expert Geoff Landis! Dr. Landis is a scientist at the NASA Glenn Research Center. He specializes in solar power systems and works on missions to Venus and Mars—including the *Pathfinder* and *Mars Exploration Rover* missions!

Question: What kinds of problems do rovers have to deal with on Mars?

Answer: It's hard to drive a rover on Mars when you have a ten- or twenty-minute delay between when you send a command and when you see what happens. It would be easy for a rover to roll up on a rock and tip over, or to get stuck in a sand dune. And at night, the surface of Mars gets colder than −100 degrees, so you have to worry about the batteries freezing.

Q: What do rover designers have to think about when building a new rover?

A: You have to think of everything at once. You have to decide how to power the rover. Solar arrays? Batteries? A nuclear power source? Then you have to decide how the rover will move. Wheels? Legs? Treads? If you want to go very fast, maybe you need to add bumpers, so it won't be a problem if you hit a rock.

Q: How does the rover's destination change the way the rover is designed?

A: If you want your rover to climb over rocks, it will need really big wheels—or maybe you should design a rover with legs, like a spider. Or make it able to fly!

Q: Can rovers "taste" or "feel"?

A: The Mars rovers have senses that are very different from ours. They have more than two eyes, and some eyes see infrared light that we don't see. This means they can see heat, which lets them tell what kinds of minerals are in rocks just by looking at them. They also have a chemical analysis laboratory on the end of an arm that they can press against a rock to find out what elements are in it.

Q: Do you grow attached to a rover?

A: I was very fond of our little *Sojourner* rover on the *Pathfinder* mission. I thought of *Sojourner* as being like a little dog that wandered around Mars and sniffed at rocks.

Q: How do you feel when you lose touch with a rover?

A: Everybody was sad when we stopped hearing from *Sojourner. Sojourner* had instructions that if it didn't hear from Earth for a week, it should drive around in big circles and look at rocks. I like to think that it roved around for a while after the last time we heard from it and explored Mars on its own.

Sojourner "sniffs" a Martian rock.

Part 3:
Life on Mars

No signs of life have been found on Mars *yet*—but the case is by no means closed! Take a look at where the search for life has led us so far.

LOWELL AND BEHOLD!

Percival Lowell
(1855–1916)

American astronomer Percival Lowell saw lines on the surface of Mars that he thought were canals. He told the world that hard-working Martians had dug huge trenches or canals to bring water from the planet's polar caps to their farmland. Pretty cool, right?

Too bad Lowell was wrong! Some of the lines Lowell saw as canals were based on real features, like Valles Marineris. Others may have been long streaks of dust blown out of craters. And in some cases, Lowell's brain simply misinterpreted the blurry, random patterns he saw through his telescope as straight lines!

SPACE VIKINGS

NASA's *Viking* landers touched down on Mars to study its surface and search for signs of life in 1976. Mini-labs inside each lander analyzed the soil and sent the results back to Earth. What did the results show? No "conclusive" or definite signs of life.

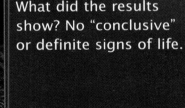

This is Lowell's map of his "canals" on Mars. The canals are the thin, dark lines, which Lowell thought were strips of irrigated farmland (because canals alone wouldn't be visible from Earth). The large shaded areas are parts of Syrtis Major, a dark region of Mars that is easily seen with a telescope.

MARS ON ICE

After the *Viking* missions, scientists discovered the first possible signs of Martian life—and guess what? They found them right here on Earth!

In 1993, scientists discovered that a meteorite found in Antarctica in 1984 had come from Mars (it was probably knocked off the Red Planet by an asteroid impact).

In 1996, scientists studying this rock (called ALH84001) found tiny globules of calcium carbonate, a material that might have been formed by living creatures. They also found tiny shapes that looked like fossils of extremely small organisms. And finally, the Mars rock contained tiny magnetic crystals very similar to ones that a certain type of bacteria creates in rocks on Earth.

These finds *could* be clues that life once existed inside this rock, way back when it was on Mars. But most scientists aren't convinced. The calcium carbonate could have been formed by chemical reactions rather than by living organisms, and the possible "fossils" are much tinier than any found on Earth. So, in the end, it's hard to know *what* to make of ALH84001!

This is ALH84001 ("ALH" stands for Allan Hills, the place in Antarctica where it was found, "84" is the year, and "001" means it was the first meteorite found that year). It's shown next to a ruler to indicate that it's about 9 inches (23 cm) long.

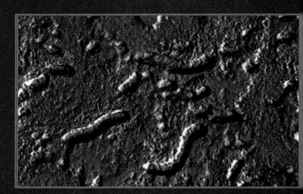

This is a super-magnified view of a cast made from the meteorite ALH84001. Some scientists think that the worm-like shapes could be fossils from tiny life forms. How tiny? The shapes are about 500 times smaller than the width of a single hair! The smallest fossils we find on Earth are much larger than this.

KEEP YOUR BRAIN PREPPED, CADET!

Don't let all the negative results and skeptics get you down or block your search for extraterrestrial life! Life can take on surprising shapes, and creatures can survive in places scientists never expected. Just think about the weird creatures that live right here on Earth in the darkest reaches of the ocean, under permanently frozen ice, or deep inside rock. Until recently, no one thought *that* kind of life existed either.

Who knows? Martian life could be something that's unlike anything we know, and we could just be looking in the wrong places for the wrong stuff. You can be sure that Earthlings will keep up the search for proof of life on Mars—so keep your eyes open for what might turn up next!

MARTIANS InVade!

On October 30, 1938, cars lined up for miles as people tried to flee their homes, and phone lines were jammed as others tried to find out what was going on. Some people wrapped their heads in towels to protect themselves from "Martian gas," and others hid in cellars. Why? According to the radio, Earth was being invaded by Martians!

RUN FOR YOUR LIFE!

A radio program produced by a famous Hollywood star and director, Orson Welles, told listeners that Martians were attacking Earthlings with deadly, unstoppable laser rays—and that New York City was in flames!

Orson Welles
(1915–1985)

Orson Welles ended the program as he started it, by letting everyone know that it was all just a Halloween story. However, many of the listeners had missed the opening warning because they tuned in late, and many missed the final announcement because they were too busy running for their lives!

GOTCHA!

These panicked people turned as red as the Red Planet when they learned the radio reports were just part of a prank. Many people didn't realize until the next day that the broadcast was a dramatic presentation of H. G. Wells's fictional tale *The War of the Worlds*. Orson Welles thought it would be more exciting if he presented the story as if it were the newscast of an actual alien invasion. Wow, was he right!

Part 4:
Destination: Mars!

HOW TO PLAN A TRIP TO THE RED PLANET

So, you want to rocket off to Mars? Robotic landers and rovers are already paving the way for humans by helping us learn more about the Red Planet. Before long, the first astronauts could be heading off to Mars! But before you hit the blastoff button, make sure you take a look at the potential problems of such a far-out trip!

PROBLEM #1: Mars is soooo far away!

POSSIBLE SOLUTION: Take the short route! Mars can be as close as 35 million miles (56 million km), when Earth passes between Mars and the Sun, or it can be as far away as *250 million miles* (400 million km), when Mars is on the far side of the Sun from us. Mars is at its closest every two years, so you'll want to make sure to time your trip just right!

A well-timed trip to Mars, using current technology, would take about seven months. Make sure to bring plenty of reading material and exercise equipment to keep your mind and body active!

PROBLEM #2: Launching a spacecraft big enough to take humans to Mars would require a lot of fuel.

POSSIBLE SOLUTION: Use a vehicle that doesn't run on traditional fuel! The kind of fuel we use for rockets nowadays, chemical fuel, is very heavy, and you need a lot of it to lift a spacecraft! Your Mars-bound spacecraft could use other types of fuel, like nuclear power, instead! You'll learn more about the possibilities of future spacecraft in *The Space Explorer's Guide to the Future in Space*!

PROBLEM #3: You could be exposed to too much radiation (from the Sun and deep space) during the trip.

POSSIBLE SOLUTION: Design your spacecraft to protect you from radiation! Another solution is to improve the way your body deals with radiation. There are drugs being tested now that help soak up radiation's effects, and some foods have been shown to be good radiation sponges, too!

Once you're on Mars, radiation exposure will *still* be a problem, because the planet's thin atmosphere won't protect you much. Radiation on Mars is about a *thousand* times stronger than on Earth! A habitat on Mars could be protected by a thin layer of soil over its walls and roof.

PROBLEM #4: The Sun, a prime energy source, is only half as strong on Mars as it is on Earth.

POSSIBLE SOLUTION: Use mirrors! These reflectors can help collect and focus the Sun's light onto solar panels, giving Mars's faint sunlight a big boost!

Another solution is to use nuclear energy. A reactor could be parked in a crater away from the settlement, where it would create a steady source of power.

A future Mars base could be made up of giant structures that hold air for people to breathe and protect them from radiation.

EXTREME MARTIAN MAKEOVER

If you can't wait to move to Mars—but aren't so thrilled about wearing a space suit and breathing from an oxygen tank whenever you head outside—then you'll see why some scientists want to *terraform* the Red Planet!

Terraforming is about creating a biosphere—or living environment—on another planet. That way, humans and plants can live on the surface without special protection. Mars is the only planet in our solar system where we could create a biosphere with our current technology. Sure, we've never tried to terraform an entire planet, but scientists have given it a lot of thought!

GET ME SOME GREENHOUSE GASES!

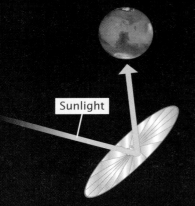

Sunlight

Some researchers think giant mirrors could be used to reflect the Sun's heat toward Mars's polar ice caps in order to melt them.

One of the first things terraformers would have to do is raise the temperature of the planet by creating a "greenhouse effect." How? Some terraformers think they could melt Mars's polar ice caps and release the carbon dioxide that's currently frozen there.

Carbon dioxide is a greenhouse gas. This means it lets sunlight pass through a planet's atmosphere, but it doesn't allow all of the rising heat to escape back into space. In other words, gases like carbon dioxide trap heat—like a greenhouse does.

Terraformers would have to be pretty patient. Even if there is enough greenhouse gas trapped in the polar ice caps to bring about the change they want, it would still take a few centuries for temps to rise to the point where Mars would be habitable.

Then the terraformers would need to introduce plants (like algae) to convert the carbon dioxide into oxygen for humans to breathe. The whole process would take thousands of years!

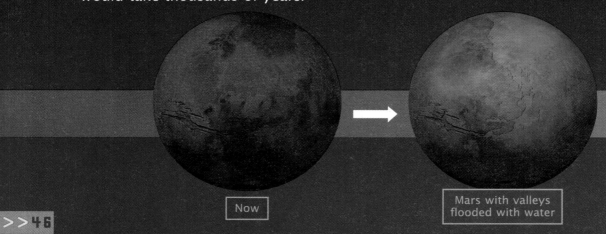

Now

Mars with valleys flooded with water

Dr. Chris McKay

PLANETARY SCIENTIST

Dr. Chris McKay, a planetary scientist at NASA's Ames Research Center, explores the possibility of life on Mars—past, present, or future!

Dr. McKay studies Mars-like environments on Earth in places like Antarctica and Siberia, and he helps plan future Mars missions (like human visits and settlements!). He's a strong supporter of the idea of *terraforming* Mars to make it habitable for life, including humans. Read on to find out his reasons why!

Question: So, do you think we should terraform Mars?

Answer: Yes! A Mars full of life is a more interesting and "valuable" planet than the beautiful but lifeless world there today.

Q: Have humans ever tried terraforming before?

A: No, but humans have demonstrated their ability to change the environment of an entire planet—Earth! Just look at global warming and the way we've harmed the ozone layer. These are two examples—negative ones—of how humans can change the environment of a planet.

Q: What's the first step? Should we try to melt Mars's polar ice caps?

A: If Mars were warmed up to temperatures suitable for life, then the polar caps would melt some. The only practical way to warm Mars that we know is to manufacture greenhouse gases on the planet. But we have to choose gases that won't destroy the ozone in Mars's atmosphere, which helps protect the planet from ultraviolet radiation.

Q: How long would it take before people could survive on the surface of Mars without special gear?

A: If you visited Mars now, you'd need a full space suit and radiation protection. In 100 years, if terraformers are able to create a thick atmosphere, you won't need a space suit or radiation protection—but you'll still need an oxygen mask. It would take terraformers about 100,000 years to get Mars to the point where you wouldn't have to wear an oxygen mask!

Q: Would all the animals, plants, soil, and extra water have to come from Earth?

A: If there is Martian life, it would be more interesting to use that! But if not, we could bring life from Earth. The water and soil would have to be Martian though—we couldn't bring enough from Earth.

Q: Thanks, Chris! Your ideas sound *terra-fic*!

The terraforming process could make Mars look like this!

Keep on
Rockin' and Rovin'

Cadet, are you "reddy" to end your Red Planet adventure? Not yet? Then stay tuned for news of future Mars missions, like these:

A and B: Instead of wheeling along the surface, airplane or balloon "rovers" could explore Mars from above!

C: This super-smart *K-9* rover can operate almost on its own, without commands from Earth.

D: The *Phoenix* lander will dig for water at Mars's north pole.

What else can Mars fans look forward to? How about a "sample return" mission, in which Martian soil and rocks would be scooped up and sent back to Earth? And, of course, there's always the long-range goal of sending *astronauts* to Mars. Could a real, live visit to the Red Planet be on *your* horizon, cadet?

Check it out... in 3-D!

THE ANSWER STATION

Page 25: **Name That Rock**
Here are the names NASA gave to some of the rocks in this area:

Half Dome
Shark
Wedge
Stump
Moe
Stimpy
Little Flat Top
Flat Top

Page 31: **Something "Bunny" Is Going On!**
The answer is B. NASA thinks these "bunny ears" are actually a piece of airbag material or something similar that fell off *Opportunity*.

Page 34: **Mars Rocks!**
The "blueberries" on Mars are actually "concretions" formed by water seeping through the Martian soil, just like in the third photo from Earth. So they're another clue for geologists that Mars once had liquid water!